ACPL I ☜ W9-DFT-484

3 1833 00579 0354

DISCARDED

PREHISTORIC WORLD

ANIMALS have lived on the earth since very ancient times. Their remains and traces, which we call fossils, reveal creatures that range from simple sea-dwellers to dinosaurs, flying reptiles, and relatives of our present-day horses, elephants, and camels.

Prehistoric World introduces young readers to typical animals of the past 350 million years. Descriptions and explanations add to the information presented in stories, and answer the question, *How do we know that prehistoric creatures looked, lived, and acted like this?*

Dr. Fenton has studied and collected fossils since he was fourteen, and is the author of technical books and articles about them. Here he draws upon his own researches and those of other scientists, right up to the fall of 1953, to bring prehistoric creatures to life in a book addressed especially to boys and girls of nine years and up, and suitable for younger readers who already know something about fossils.

Books by Carroll Lane Fenton

LIFE LONG AGO: THE STORY OF FOSSILS
ALONG THE HILL
EARTH'S ADVENTURES:
The Story of Geology for Young People
ALONG NATURE'S HIGHWAY
WEEJACK AND HIS NEIGHBORS
WILD FOLK AT THE POND
WILD FOLK IN THE WOODS
PREHISTORIC WORLD

By Carroll Lane Fenton and Mildred Adams Fenton

WORLDS IN THE SKY
RICHES FROM THE EARTH

FRONTISPIECE: *Brontosaurus, the "Thunder Lizard." Here we see this huge dinosaur as he would have looked if he had been able to walk on land. The plants around him are horsetails, also called scouring rushes. (Painting by James E. Allen, courtesy of the Sinclair Refining Co., Inc.)*

PREHISTORIC WORLD

STORIES OF ANIMAL LIFE IN PAST AGES

BY CARROLL LANE FENTON

WITH DRAWINGS BY THE AUTHOR

Color plates by James E. Allen

j 5-60
F 36p

THE JOHN DAY COMPANY, NEW YORK

COPYRIGHT, 1954, BY CARROLL LANE FENTON

All rights reserved. This book, or parts thereof, must not be reproduced in any form without permission. Published by The John Day Company, 62 West 45th Street, New York 36, N.Y., and on the same day in Canada by Longmans, Green & Company, Toronto.

Library of Congress Catalog Card Number: 54-5884

Sixth Impression

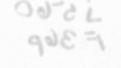

MANUFACTURED IN THE UNITED STATES OF AMERICA

CONTENTS

U. S. 1166781

Chart of "Prehistoric" Ages

Eras	Ages	Events Among Living Things
CENOZOIC, or "ERA OF MAMMALS" Began 70 million years ago; has not come to an end.	Recent	Man became dominant, using and killing many other animals.
	Ice Age	Glaciers spread widely on northern continents. Mammoths and other animals wandered to and fro.
	Tertiary	Mammals grew common and developed into most of the groups living today and others that have died out.
MESOZOIC, or "ERA OF REPTILES". Began 200 million years ago; lasted 130 million years.	Chalk Age, or Cretaceous	New kinds of dinosaurs and other reptiles appeared, but died out as the Chalk Age ended.
	Jurassic	Dinosaurs became giants; flying and swimming reptiles were common, and birds developed.
	Triassic	Dinosaurs and beast-reptiles appeared, as well as many other reptiles.
PALEOZOIC, or "ERA OF ANCIENT LIFE" Began 500 million years ago; lasted 300 million years.	Permian	Reptiles first became common. Some amphibians were very large.
	Coal Age, or Carboniferous	Great swampy forests grew in many places.
	Devonian	Fish became common; some of them turned into amphibians.
	Silurian	Trilobites, horn-shells, corals, and many other creatures without backbones were common in seas.
	Ordovician	
	Cambrian	
PROTEROZOIC and ARCHEOZOIC Began at least 3 billion years ago.		Ages in these eras are not well known. Fossils are rare except for masses made by simple plants.

6

Fossil snails, oysterlike shells, and a clam. All are petrified and are very ancient, or "prehistoric."

TALES TOLD BY SHELLS

AGES upon ages ago, a snail lived on the bottom of a shallow sea. There the snail crawled about on one broad foot that really was the under side of its body. When the creature was hungry, it ate small plants. When it was frightened, it tucked itself into a hard, coiled shell.

The snail lived in this way for several years, but at last it died. Its soft flesh soon disappeared, but its shell lay upon the sea bottom among other dead shells. Mud filled the empty coils, and more mud settled upon them. It formed a closely packed layer that kept the shells from being destroyed.

As hundreds and thousands of years went by, many more layers of mud settled and turned into rocks such as shale and limestone. In time the shallow sea disappeared and the layers of rock were pushed up into land.

While these changes were going on, others took place in the shells. Their bright colors first were destroyed. Then water that soaked through the rocks left tiny bits of minerals. In this way the shells were petrified, or "turned into stone." Many became harder than the rocks that covered them.

We often call the petrified shells *prehistoric,* for they lived and died long before written history began. But a better name for them is *fossils.* A fossil is the remains or trace of something that lived during an ancient part of the earth's history. This history, which is told in rocks instead of in writing, is a very long one. It begins about 10 thousand years ago and goes back more than 3 billion years.

. . . .

Countless fossils are petrified, but many others are not. Some shells and bones that were covered with clay or fine sand have not become stony. Other unchanged bones are found in caves or in deposits of tar that oozed up to the surface. Near the end of the Ice Age, hairy elephants sometimes fell into cracks in the ice and stayed there until their bodies were frozen. These frozen fossils still have their flesh, skin and hair. Even food which the ancient elephants were eating is sometimes found in their mouths.

In many places, both plants and animals were covered by mud so fine that it kept them from decaying completely. Their remains became films of black coaly material called carbon. These films show the forms of many plants, as well as the skin and flesh of some animals.

In beds of sandstone and other coarse rocks, fossil hunters often find impressions of shells, stems and leaves. Though the actual remains have decayed, these impressions also are fossils. So is stony material made from mud or sand that hardened in ancient shells.

Bones, shells and fallen leaves were dead, but some fossils were made by creatures while they were still alive. Dinosaurs (dy' no saurz), for example, walked on wet sand or mud, leaving footprints that were preserved when the mud or sand became stone. Snails crawled upon sea bottoms, making trails that now wind across layers of rock. Worms dug burrows and filled them with sand, which shows as plainly as it did ages ago. And

9

some rough pits tell us that other sea dwellers dug up worms for food.

These are not all the types of fossils, but they are the most important. Scientists have arranged them according to their relationships—snails with snails, reptiles with reptiles, and so on. You'd never guess how many different groups of animals and plants have been discovered as fossils.

Scientists also have arranged fossils according to their age. They begin with remains and traces from very ancient times, and end with things that lived only 10 to 20 thousand years ago. This arrangement tells the story of life through the earth's long history.

We can't tell that whole story in one book, for the tale is much too long. But we can pick out a few important chapters, and some of the most important creatures. We also can describe some of the plants among which those creatures lived. This will leave out many details, but it will tell much about living things during many long ages and many millions of years.

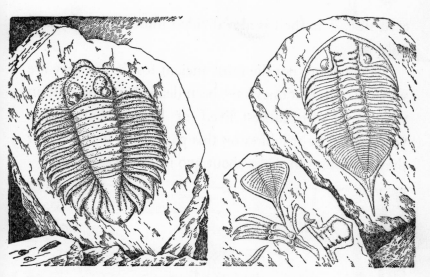

Two fossil trilobites. Beside one of them are pieces from some empty shells.

HOW TRILOBITES LIVED

THE fossils on these slabs of stone are petrified shells of creatures related to lobsters and horseshoe crabs. Since they have no common English name, we call them trilobites (try′ lo bites), which means "three-lobed creatures." As you can see, one part (or lobe) runs lengthwise through the middle of the shell, with another lobe on each side. The shell is also divided into head, body and tail.

Trilobites are not the most ancient fossils, but they are very old. The last ones have been dead about 200 million years, and the earliest lived at least a half billion years ago. The trilobites on this page came between, for they are found in rocks about 350 million years old.

The trilobites shown on page eleven looked like this when they were alive and crawled upon the bottom of a sea.

Shall we put on imaginary diving helmets and visit the ancient sea in which these creatures lived?

The first things we notice are seaweeds that wave to and fro. Then we find a trilobite. It is broad and has a rough shell, like the fossil on our left-hand stone.

The living trilobite crawls on many jointed legs attached to the under side of its body. Its broad shell is jointed, too, and so are the antennae, or "feelers," at the front of its head. The trilobite uses its feelers to smell out food. They work much better than its eyes, which are near the back of its head. They look upward, sidewise or backward, but they cannot see small things lying upon the bottom.

As the trilobite crawls along it comes to some sea lilies and sea nuts. They look like plants growing upon

A trilobite wriggling out of a shell that has become too small for his growing body.

jointed stalks, but they really are creatures related to starfish. They wave their arms to and fro to capture food, which consists of tiny things that swim and float in the water. When sea lilies die they often go to pieces, and the sections of their stalks look like flat beads. In some places these "beads" are so common that they fill beds of stone.

Soon the rough-shelled trilobite meets another—the one with a pointed head and a spine on its tail. The eyes of this creature are made up of many sections, like the eyes of a fly. The sections are covered with a smooth layer that often disappears from fossils.

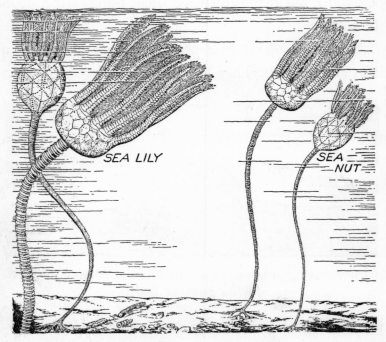

Crinoids, or sea lilies, and two sea nuts. All were animals distantly related to starfish.

Both trilobites are hungry, but they do not attack each other. One finds some small dead animals, and the other

FACING PAGE *This duckbill dinosaur had a rounded crest of bone on his head. (Courtesy of the Sinclair Refining Company, Inc.)*

digs worms from the mud. Each trilobite uses specially shaped legs to push food into its mouth, which is on the under side of its head.

Anything that eats must grow, and trilobites grow rapidly. But the shells that cover them cannot stretch or be made larger. This means that a growing trilobite is

Trilobites that swam, crawled in mud, and rolled up when danger threatened.

squeezed inside a shell that becomes tighter and tighter. At last it splits open on the head and lets the animal creep out.

A trilobite that has shed its shell is soft, like a modern "soft-shell" crab. It hides away among seaweeds while its body rapidly becomes larger and a new shell forms like a crust on its skin. The old shell is left on the sea bottom, where currents often break it to pieces. We see some of these pieces half buried in mud. There they will probably lie until they become fossils.

Coming back from our imaginary trip, we look at several fossil trilobites to find out how they lived. Some are broad and almost flat. They probably dug their tails into the sea bottom and waited for dead food to drift close to their mouths. Others skimmed over the bottom or even swam, but species with round heads and tails plowed along in the mud and dug worms for food.

Little trilobites with many long spines lived among tangles of seaweeds or drifted in the water. When danger threatened they flipped their legs and quickly swam away.

Many small thick-shelled trilobites had a still better way of escaping danger. When something alarmed one of them it rolled up, bringing its head and tail together. Jointed sections protected the rest of the body and completely covered the legs. An "enrolled" trilobite was as safe as an old-time knight in his suit of armor with a helmet on his head. In spite of this the animals sometimes died, for their rolled-up shells are found among other fossils.

HORN-SHELL AND HIS NEIGHBORS

SHALL we take another imaginary trip into an ancient sea? This one spread across eastern Canada and the United States about 300 million years ago. It left

FOSSIL

Horn-shell has caught a trilobite and is pulling it to his mouth.

deposits of limestone and shale that contain great numbers of fossils.

We soon notice a place where seaweeds are shaking and the water is cloudy with mud. Then we see a large, smooth shell that looks like a closely coiled horn. It belongs to a soft, pink creature with two large eyes and many tentacles, or arms. They are coiled around a trilobite that is trying to get away.

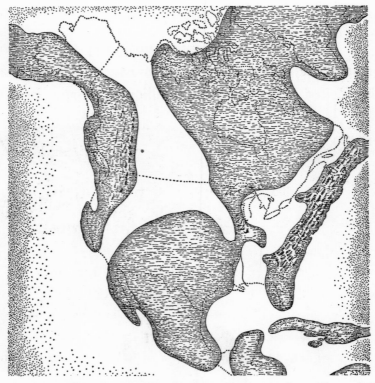

A map of North America during the age when Horn-shell lived.

The trilobite struggles and twists, but the pink arms hold it tightly and pull it to Horn-shell's mouth. He bites the trilobite with two sharp beaks and then eats its flesh. When his meal is over he crawls away, until something alarms him. Then Horn-shell takes water into his body and shoots it out through a tube on the under side of his head. The jets of water make him swim backward, with his shell in front of his body and arms.

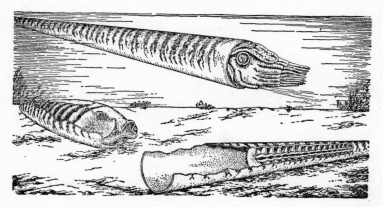

These broken shells show the partitions that divide them into sections.

These arms and the two big eyes tell us that Horn-shell is related to the modern squid and octopus, though they do not have shells. All belong to the mollusks, a group of soft-bodied animals that also includes clams, oysters and snails.

As Horn-shell swims backward or crawls about, he meets other relatives. They are not horn shaped, however, for their shells are straight and come to a point, like slender ice-cream cones. Broken shells show that each one is made up of sections, or chambers, separated by curved layers. At the end of each shell is a much larger "living chamber" which covered the soft body, with its eyes and arms.

Though brachiopods built thick shells, their bodies were very small.

Horn-shell preys on his own relatives, as well as on trilobites. But he never tries to eat creatures which we call brachiopods (brak′ i o pods), for their bodies are too small. In spite of this they build thick shells with many different shapes. The thin ones lie on the sea bottom, but many thick kinds have tough stalks that burrow into the mud. These stalks keep currents of water from rolling the shells about. Still other thick brachiopods sink into the mud so deeply that they cannot move.

Even when Horn-shell is very hungry he does not eat the corals that live in his ancient sea.

People often call corals "insects," but that is a mistake. Corals are creatures whose bodies look like soft, round tubes with rings of tentacles at the top. Most corals also

Corals of various kinds that lived in Horn-shell's sea.

build stony supports, or bases, that keep them out of the mud.

Some of the corals that live in Horn-shell's sea have bases that look like small, wrinkled horns. Others build dome-shaped masses or branched supports covered with ridges and pits. One coral lives on top of each horn, but dozens live together in the dome-shaped and branched colonies. Still more are found in colonies that look like stony honeycombs. When all these corals grow close together, they build up so many bases that they form layers of rock.

.   .   .   .

The words "layers of rock" remind us that Horn-shell and his neighbors are fossils. They lived and died long ages ago, in a sea that covered places which are now dry land. We find them in beds of limestone and shale, or pick them up where rain has washed them out of clay-banks. We also find other fossils that resemble them, although they lived in different seas during different ages. Their kinds will not be the same, of course, but they still will be horn-shells, brachiopods and corals that are shaped like horns, branches or honeycombs.

Lobe-fin could crawl out of the water when it was filled with dead, decaying plants.

FROM FINS TO LEGS

WHILE Horn-shell hunted trilobites, a blunt-headed fish swam in a pond in the country now known as Scotland. Scientists have given this fish a long name made from two Greek words that mean "lobe-fin."

Lobe-fin was not large, and he was not beautiful. His colors were dull green or brownish, like those of most fish that live in ponds. His blunt head was covered with thick bony plates, and rows of bony scales ran along his body. His backbone curved upward and went to the end of his tail, just as the backbone does in sharks. There were two fins on his back and one beneath, and four more fins formed pairs on his sides. These paired fins ex-

23

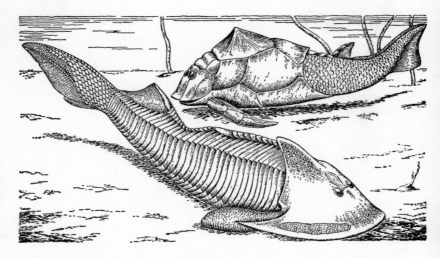

The fishlike creature with electric organs on its head. Near it is an armored wing-fish.

plained Lobe-fin's name, for each one was like a fringe fastened to a thick base, or lobe.

Though Lobe-fin was not very active, he had a big appetite. He spent much of his time hunting for food, which he snapped up with sharp teeth on his upper and lower jaws. Sometimes he snapped so hard that he broke off a tooth. The broken end showed that the hard outer layer, or enamel, was deeply crumpled into the tooth.

Lobe-fin fed upon other fish, some of which were young lobe-fins. He did not bother queer fishlike creatures that had bony heads shaped like a half-moon and rings of jointed bone around their bodies. These creatures swam or wriggled over the bottom of the pond, eating worms and other small animals which they found on the mud. They balanced their bodies with two flaplike fins, and when something attacked them they gave it a shock with electric organs which looked like rough places near the edges of their heads. Lobe-fin had learned to avoid those painful electric shocks.

Another creature that was safe from Lobe-fin has a name that means "wing-fish." Wing-fish was a stubby creature less than six inches long, with solid plates of bone on its head and body and thick, rounded scales on its tail. It also wriggled over the bottom or crawled by means of its "wings." These really were two slender fins covered with bony plates like those on the head.

．　　．　　．　　．

The land around Lobe-fin's pond was bare and mountainous. Hard rains often fell in the winter and spring, filling ponds and sending so much water into rivers that they overflowed. Summers brought long droughts, when rain did not fall for weeks or months. At such times many rivers ran dry, while ponds became shallow pools or even disappeared.

These droughts were very hard on Wing-fish and the creatures with electric organs on their heads. Some lived for a while in ponds that grew smaller and smaller, but died when the ponds became foul with dead, decaying plants. Others were stranded on banks of sand and mud when the water evaporated.

Lobe-fin and other fish related to him did not have such a hard time. When water in small ponds became foul, these fish swam to the surface and gulped mouthfuls of air. This air went into simple lungs, which breathed just as well as gills. Lobe-fin could breathe air for months, until rains fell again and filled his pond with fresh, pure water.

Even when ponds dried up, the lobe-finned fish were not helpless. Most of them wriggled out of the mud and began to crawl toward other ponds that still contained a little water. They crawled with the thick lobes of their fins, which contained both muscles and bones.

Some of these lobe-fins died as they crawled over banks of sand and dry mud. Others kept on going until they found streams or ponds that still contained some water. The tired fish pushed themselves into the water and there lived safely till the next rainy season.

. . . .

This process went on year after year, for thousands of centuries. Each year, fish that had the largest, strongest

This ancient amphibian from Greenland had stubby legs and a fishlike tail.

fin lobes lived, since they could crawl to water. But fish with weak, short lobes died when they tried to travel on land.

Something else happened, too; something of great importance. Some fish with long, strong lobes laid eggs that grew into young fish which were larger than their parents. They also developed longer fin lobes, with thicker bones and stronger muscles. Some of the bones even changed shape and began to resemble bones in legs, not fins.

This also happened again and again, during thousands of centuries. At last some fish laid eggs that hatched into creatures that had real legs and feet. They also breathed with gills only when they were young. After that they used lungs and let their gills disappear. Since these creatures could live either on land or in water, we call them amphibians (am fib′ i ans).

Fossils discovered in Greenland show what one of the first amphibians was like. It was a big creature four to five feet long, with a skull containing bones like those in the skull of Lobe-fin. It also had teeth with deeply crumpled enamel and a long, fishlike tail. But the fins on its back and under side were gone, and its legs ended in feet with stubby toes.

This amphibian still spent most of its time in the water, where it swam by means of its tail. But when dry seasons came it could crawl from one pond or stream to another much faster than any fish. This helped it to live during an age when seas turned into land, low land became mountains, and ponds or streams ran dry almost every summer.

Cacops often walked on land, though his children were tad-poles that lived in a pool.

SOME ANCIENT AMPHIBIANS

WE now skip more than 20 million years, to a part of earth history called the Permian period. It came just after the Carboniferous, or Coal, Age when plants that grew in many great swamps died and formed beds of coal.

One morning the sun shone brightly on a low, swampy delta in what now is northern Texas. Trees that looked like huge moss plants grew beside streams, and tall ferns that had seeds on their leaves formed thickets. Dragonflies almost two feet wide zoomed through the air or rested on tall horsetail rushes whose leaves were arranged in rings. All these plants were related to those of the Coal Age swamps.

A rustling sound among the ferns was made by an amphibian. He was a thick-bodied creature about sixteen inches long, with short legs and a stubby tail. Lumps of bone ran down the middle of his back and his jaws contained many sharp teeth that had crumpled enamel. He showed them plainly when he caught a roach almost three inches in length.

The amphibian, called Cacops (kay′ kops), blinked his eyes as he swallowed the roach. Then he crawled to a fallen tree, looking for other insects. When he found one he gulped it down and went on through the woods.

If Cacops had looked into a pool, he might have seen some of his children. They were plump creatures with long tails and legs that were just beginning to grow. They breathed with gills that looked like dark frills, just behind their heads.

But Cacops was not interested in his children, and did not even know they were his. They had hatched from eggs laid by his mate, early in the spring. The eggs were round balls much smaller than marbles, and were covered with sticky jelly that fastened them to sticks in the pool. Cacops and his mate went away as soon as the eggs

Diplocaulus had a broad bony head, a slender body, and legs so small that they were almost useless.

were fastened down. The young ones took care of themselves, eating small water plants until they could catch worms and insects for food.

· · · ·

Several other amphibians also lived in the streams and ponds of that ancient Texas delta. The strangest of these was Diplocaulus (dip′ lo kaw″ lus), a flat-bodied creature almost three feet long, with a wide bony head that ended in points. Diplocaulus swam with his tail, for his little legs were weak and useless. The creature spent his whole life in the water, often lying in one spot for hours or even for days at a time. He also never quite grew up, for he never breathed with lungs. He used gills that were covered by folds of skin, just behind his head.

31

Eryops was hunting in a swampy stream.

Diplocaulus did wake up and swim away when Eryops (air′ ee ops) came near. Eryops looked a bit like a huge, long-tailed Cacops five to seven feet in length. He had a broad, flattened head, a barrel-shaped body, and a tail that was longer than his head. His legs were thick and strong, but were much too short to lift his body from the ground. He could swim and dive swiftly in the water, but crawled on land so clumsily that he never went very far.

On the day Cacops crept through the woods, a large Eryops went hunting in a swampy stream. He dived several times after Diplocaulus, who always managed to get away. Then Eryops ate several fish, catching them between sharp teeth which also had crumpled enamel.

32

Those teeth showed that both Eryops and Cacops were related to the earliest amphibians.

Next Eryops swam toward a bank where ferns and horsetails came down to the edge of the stream. There he floated near the surface, while the sunshine warmed his rough skin. His nose and eyes were above water, so he could breathe and watch the shore.

Eryops was ready to catch some defenseless creature as it came out of the woods. When he heard a noise he slipped still closer and got ready to snap his jaws.

As he did so, he saw something big rush toward him. He also saw a big mouth filled with teeth that looked like daggers. Eryops swung his tail and pulled back just in time to keep those teeth from slashing his neck.

Eryops did not pause to find out what had attacked him. He swam backward for several feet, turned his big body and dived. Then he swam away under water to the center of the stream. There he paused for a while to rest, lying so quietly on the bottom that he did not need to breathe. But at last some fish swam overhead, and the big amphibian's stomach reminded him that he still was hungry. Eryops swung his tail and swam toward the surface to hunt another meal.

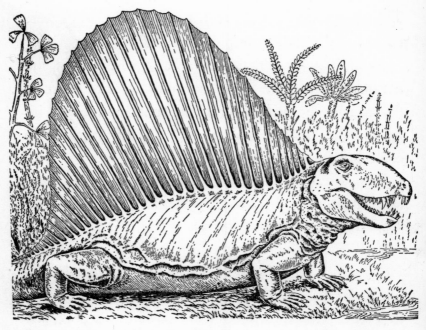

Finback's long teeth showed that he fed on other animals.

FINBACK OF ANCIENT TEXAS

THE creature that frightened Eryops stopped at
the edge of the water and gave an angry grunt. Then
he turned and walked away through the rushes.

He made a lot of noise as he went, for he was very
large and clumsy. His length was eleven feet, and he
weighed more than six hundred fifty pounds. His legs

were strong and his body was thick, and long spines of bone grew up above his back. They were covered with a web of skin and explained his common name, which is Finback.

Finback's head showed that he had a bad temper, and that he fed on meat. Near the front of his mouth were long, sharp teeth which were just right for slashing. Back of these were smaller teeth with serrate, or sawlike, edges. Finback used these sawlike teeth to cut chunks of meat from his prey.

U. S. 1166781

. . . .

Although Finback was a savage meat-eater he did not prowl through the woods or follow the trails of other creatures until he could kill them. Beasts such as wolves hunt in that way, but Finback was a reptile with cold blood and a small, stupid brain. He was too dull to follow his prey for hours, and he soon became tired when he ran. He had to use an easier way of capturing his food.

What Finback did was very simple. He went through the woods till he found a trail on which other creatures often traveled. There he stopped and kept quite still, often for several hours. But when something came, he rushed forward and killed it with his long sharp teeth.

Finback had been waiting near a trail when Eryops swam into shallow water. But Eryops had escaped, so

Finback went back to the forest and hid beside a thicket of ferns.

There he stayed for a long time, waiting for something to come. Dragonflies hummed overhead, and big roaches scrambled among the ferns. They would have made a fine meal for Cacops, but Finback did not eat insects.

At last another reptile appeared—a reptile that looked like a huge lizard with a wide body, a thick tail and a short, heavy head. Finback waited till this reptile came close and dashed toward it. *Snap!* went his jaws on the other's neck. Next he gave it several crunching bites. Then Finback grunted in satisfaction and began to devour his victim.

The dead reptile weighed almost two hundred pounds, which was more meat than even Finback could eat at just one meal. He filled his stomach and settled down for a nap, but woke up when another finbacked reptile tried to take some of the meat. Finback opened his mouth and roared hoarsely till the other reptile went away.

It was afternoon of the next day when Finback woke up again. By that time the meat was beginning to spoil, but Finback did not mind. He gulped down such large bites that he sometimes had to twist and turn to get them down his throat. Like other reptiles, both ancient and modern, Finback did not chew his food.

When Finback had eaten all he could he went to sleep again. When he woke up he sniffed at the spoiled meat. But instead of eating, he yawned and crawled along the trail through the woods.

This time Finback saw several other reptiles. Some looked like lizards four or five feet long, with short legs, long tails and pointed snouts. Others were relatives of Finback, and had fins that resembled his. Still, the bony spines on those fins had short, blunt crossbars, and the creatures had small heads. Their teeth also were small and blunt, which showed that they fed on plants, not meat.

The plant-eaters were munching ferns, nipping off the juicy stalks that had not spread out into leaves. Then they stopped eating and listened, for a savage creature just like Finback was slowly crawling through the ferns. They scrambled away as it rushed toward them, but its teeth broke some of the spines in one plant-eater's fin. In time the broken spines would heal, but they would not grow straight. They would bend over as long as the reptile lived, and would show plainly when its bones finally were petrified.

This other finbacked reptile showed how the strange fin was used. The reptile had been in shady woods and was cool. It turned broadside to the sun, letting its fin

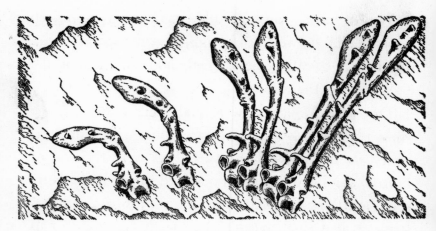

These spines of a plant-eating reptile were broken when a reptile like Finback tried to kill him.

soak up the sunshine, which soon warmed its body. But when the creature felt warm enough it turned so sunlight shone on the edge of its fin, making little heat.

Finback himself became hot when he left the woods and crawled across an open flat covered with steaming mud. When he came to the woods again he stopped where a breeze was blowing and stubby trees made shade. There his fin began to lose heat, which went into the air. This made Finback feel just right. He blinked his eyes and settled down for a nap. He might sleep for a day or two, until his stomach became empty and told him to hunt another meal.

We have called Finback a reptile, but Cacops was an amphibian. Yet both were four-legged creatures that lived on land. What was the difference between them?

We can tell reptiles from amphibians by their bones, but the greatest difference is in their ways of living. Although many grown-up amphibians live upon land, most of them start their lives in the water. That is where the females lay their eggs, and it is where the young ones stay as long as they breathe with gills, like fish. In fact, some amphibians no longer breathe with lungs. This means that they have to stay in the water, like Diplocaulus, even when they become full grown.

Reptiles never breathe with gills, and they never lay their eggs in the water. Reptile eggs have their own moisture, and are laid on land or kept in the mother's body till they hatch. The little ones also breathe with lungs, just as their parents do. That is true even of reptiles like turtles, which go to live in water a short time *after* they hatch.

Long-jaw looked like a huge crocodile, but his nostrils were close to his eyes.

LONG-JAW AND EARLY DINOSAURS

A FEW million years after Finback lived, the earth went through such great changes that we call them a revolution. Shallow seas disappeared, low lands were pushed upward, and rocks crumpled into mountains. Some of these mountains began in what now is Alabama and extended to northeastern Canada. In other places great sheets of ice called glaciers (glay′ shers) covered the ground. They caused climates as cold as the weather of Greenland in places that had been warm.

This revolution brought an end to one era and began

another. It also caused the death of Finback, Eryops and many other animals. When the earth settled down and grew warm again, new kinds of reptiles became common. Some looked and acted like crocodiles and lizards. Others became the creatures we now call dinosaurs.

These new reptiles lived in many parts of the world. When some died their bones were petrified, but others left only footprints on mud or sand that hardened into stone. Those fossil footprints are most common in the eastern part of North America. They were often found in the days when people quarried "brownstone" to make buildings in towns and in cities such as New York.

Although fossil footprints are common in the East, the best place to find bones of reptiles that made them is in northern Arizona. There we also may see the logs and stumps of trees among which the reptiles lived. The finest logs and stumps now form the famous Petrified Forest near the town of Holbrook. Thousands of people visit it every year.

We must use our imaginations to see this forest as it looked about 150 million years ago. It grew on low, moist ground where rivers wound among trees that looked like tall pines. After long hard rains the rivers became floods which washed trees downstream and left them on banks of sticky mud. At other times small volcanoes erupted. They sent out clouds of steam and ash that settled upon both mudbanks and woods.

.   .   .   .

Near one mudbank the water rippled over something that resembled a log twenty-five or thirty feet long. But suddenly the "log" began to move, showing that it was a reptile with a slender snout, four short legs, and a flattened tail with which it swam. It looked and acted like a crocodile, but its nostrils were just in front of its eyes. The nostrils of a crocodile are near the end of its snout.

An early scientist called this animal a phytosaur (fy′ toe saur), or "plant lizard," because he thought it fed upon plants. We now know that its food consisted of fish, with amphibians and other reptiles when it was able to catch them. Since its technical name does not really fit it, suppose we call the creature Long-jaw. Those words do give a good idea of its head.

Long-jaw swallowed his food while he was in the water. Then he swam to a mudbank and crawled out. He liked to lie and rest on mudbanks while sunshine made him warm.

As Long-jaw lay on the mud he saw several other reptiles. One was about fifteen feet long, with bony plates on its back and along its tail. Thick spines of bone protected its sides, and there were five pairs of bony spikes

This reptile, about thirty inches long, was the ancestor of true crocodiles.

on its neck and above its forelegs. Its head was not as large as Long-jaw's and its teeth showed that it did eat plants, not fish or meat. It half swam and half waded in shallow places. There it could find plenty of food, and Long-jaw could not reach it.

Another creature which Long-jaw saw was the great-great-grandfather of true crocodiles. It was a reptile about thirty inches long, with large eyes, a pointed head, and nostrils near the end of its snout. Broad plates of bone covered its back and tail, as well as the under side of its body.

Though this little crocodile could swim, it often walked through the woods and across sandy uplands. Since its hind legs were longer than its forelegs, it could go uphill easily. But coming downhill was harder. Some-

*These early, or primitive, dinosaurs walked on their hind legs
and balanced themselves with their tails.*

times the reptile looked as if it were going to roll over
on its head.

. . . . .

When the crocodile traveled overland it often met
some of the first American dinosaurs.

In spite of their name, which means "terrible lizards,"
these reptiles were not big or fierce. One kind, in fact,
was only six feet long and weighed forty to fifty pounds.
It had a high, narrow head, a slender neck, and a body
that resembled a chicken with wrinkled skin instead of

feathers. Its forelegs were short and it walked and ran upon its hind legs, which were long and slender. A tail that stuck out stiffly served as a balance for its body.

These small dinosaurs did not live in thick forests, where trees grew close together and were very large. Hunting was better in groves and small thickets, where small reptiles and amphibians were common. The dinosaurs had long jaws and many sharp teeth, which were just right for catching small food.

One day, while the crocodile dozed near a pond, some larger meat-eating reptiles attacked the dinosaurs. One hissed with pain and disappeared, but the others began to run. For a moment they bobbed awkwardly. Then they dashed away swiftly, with their bodies tipped forward and their tails stretched out behind.

The crocodile did not watch them go, and he did not try to see what had scared them. Instead, he raised himself up on his hind legs and dived into the pond. There he swam to a clump of water plants and stopped with only his eyes and nostrils above water. He could float there without being seen, even if the savage hunters should come close to his pond.

THE SLEEPY "THUNDER LIZARD"

BRONTO opened his eyes and made a sound that was half way between a hiss and a roar. Something had wakened him from his nap, and he felt angry.

Bronto's full name was Brontosaurus (bron″ toe saw′ rus), which means "thunder lizard." He really was a huge dinosaur that lived about 40 million years after Long-jaw swam in Arizona. His home was a swamp that dried up long ago. Mud and sand that filled the swamp now form beds of stone among the Rocky Mountains.

Bronto did not know about the Rocky Mountains or even about his name. But he did know that some other creature was splashing and grunting so loudly that he could not sleep. He raised his head to see who it was, and gave another hissing roar.

Though Bronto's head was small and blunt, his neck was very long. When he stretched it he could see far out across the water. He could look over the palmlike trees and big horsetail rushes that grew in the swamp.

When Bronto raised his long neck he could look far across the swamp.

Behind Bronto's neck came a huge body with four massive legs, and a tail that was thick at the base but almost as thin as a whip at the end. His whole length was more than seventy feet, and he weighed about thirty-five tons, or ten times as much as a good-sized elephant.

As Bronto raised his head he saw the creature that had disturbed him. It was another kind of dinosaur, with a slim snaky neck and a whiplash tail that was even longer than Bronto's. But this reptile's head looked small and weak, and her nostrils were higher than her eyes. When she wanted to do so, she could breathe with most of her head under water.

Long-tail, or Diplodocus (dip lod' o cus), was moving her tail and splashing so hard that she did not hear Bronto's first roar. When he roared again, she did hear and looked at him in alarm. As he started toward her, she hurried away, with her long tail trailing behind. She was big, but not big enough to quarrel with an angry thunder lizard!

Bronto watched Long-tail go, but he did not follow her. By that time he was wide awake and not so angry, while an empty feeling in his stomach meant that he needed a meal. He forgot Long-tail and walked to a place where thick juicy plants almost filled the swamp. Down went his head to get a mouthful, which he swallowed with a sucking sound.

Bronto pulled up many mouthfuls of plants—twenty or thirty bushels of them. He gulped the plants down without chewing, and did not mind when good-sized stones were fastened to the roots. In fact, Bronto often swallowed stones on purpose, for they helped his stomach grind his food after he swallowed it. Even meat-eating dinosaurs made use of such "gizzard stones."

After Bronto finished his dinner, he stood still for a long time. The sun shone on his back and sides, warming his huge body. Since he was cold blooded, like all other reptiles, he needed heat from the sun.

The big dinosaur stood so long that he became drowsy and then went to sleep. He slept all the rest of the day, but woke up just before sunset. He saw the sky turn orange-red and went to sleep again.

Those long sleeps did not mean that Bronto was really tired. The big dinosaur, as you know, was a reptile—and reptiles often sleep after eating their meals. Even when they do not sleep they may stand or lie in one place for hours without moving their heads, their tails, or their legs.

When Bronto woke up next morning he ate a few more mouthfuls of plants. Then he heard swishing and bumping sounds in the woods at the edge of the swamp. Up went Bronto's head in alarm, while his forefeet dug into the mud and his hind legs pushed his body forward. His big shoulders stirred the water into waves as he hurried to a safe place far out in the swamp.

Bronto had no real need to be alarmed, for the sounds

Stegosaurus was a land-dwelling dinosaur that had armor plates on his back and four sharp spikes on his tail.

were made by Stegosaurus (steg″ o saw′ rus), a dinosaur that lived on dry land instead of in the swamp. Stegosaurus was about twenty feet long and twelve feet high, and he weighed eight or nine tons. His body was deep but thin, his hind legs were longer than his forelegs, and three toes on each of his feet ended in hoof-shaped claws. His broad sides were covered with leathery skin that contained lumps of bone. Two rows of bony plates also ran from his head to his tail, which was armed with four sharp spikes.

Most armored animals were peaceful, and that was true of Stegosaurus. He ate leaves of ferns and low trees, nipping them off with beaks on his upper and lower jaws. If something attacked him, he turned his back, with its armor plates of bone. He also protected himself with his tail, which jerked and swung from side to side the moment anything touched it. Stegosaurus could strike hard blows with his tail without bothering to think about it. Perhaps he did not even know that his tail was swinging those four big spikes against an enemy.

Bronto soon got over his fright, but he kept on wading through the swamp. At first he walked on all four feet, with his tail dragging on the bottom. Then his tail began to float, and so did his huge body. By that time Bronto walked only on his forefeet, kicking with his hind legs as if he were trying to swim. Sometimes he kicked so hard that his claws dug through the mud on the bottom of the swamp.

Even when Bronto walked on four feet he never tried to leave the water. His legs were both big and strong but their joints were formed by pads of soft cartilage instead of hard bone. The cartilage worked very well in a swamp, where the water supported a large part of Bronto's enormous weight. But his joints would have been crushed and torn if he had tried to walk on land.

As Bronto half waded and half swam through the

Allosaurus was the largest, most savage dinosaur in the forests near Bronto's swamp.

swamp, he saw some dinosaurs about twenty feet long that were feeding in shallow water near the shore. They seemed to be afraid of something, for they swallowed plants one mouthful at a time and then listened for danger. When one of them grunted they all stopped eating and hurried out into the swamp. They did so just in time, for a meat-eating dinosaur came crashing out of the woods.

Many meat-eaters are much smaller than the animals they kill, but this one was about thirty-five feet long. It had a large head and eighty long sharp teeth. Its hind legs were long and powerful, and its toes were armed with big curved claws. They could be used to hold prey while the teeth tore off chunks of meat.

This creature, known as Allosaurus (al″ o saw′ rus), was the largest and most savage dinosaur in the forests near Bronto's swamp. It sometimes ate dead reptiles that were washed ashore, but it also hunted living reptiles in forests and in swamps that had firm bottoms. Since its feet were not built for swimming or wading, it could not go far into swamps whose bottoms were covered with very soft mud. As soon as Allosaurus felt his feet begin to sink deeply, he turned and went back to the land.

By that time the plant-eaters were far away, in water so deep that only their heads showed above the surface. Bronto was in deep water too. There he stood quite still until he felt hungry again. Since he already was far from shore he waded still farther to a place where plants grew around an island.

Once again Bronto ate as much as he could, swallowing still more stones to help grind the food in his stomach. Then he went back to deep water, planted all four feet on the bottom and went to sleep again. Unless some other dinosaur disturbed him, he probably would not move until he needed another meal.

.   .   .   .

Scientists used to think that Allosaurus and other large meat-eating dinosaurs almost never went into the water. Then a collector found the footprints of a Brontosaurus that waded through a coastal marsh in what now is northern Texas. Near those huge tracks were smaller ones made by Allosaurus or one of his relatives. He must have waded through water at least eight feet deep as he followed the trail of Brontosaurus.

These fossil footprints, as well as a skeleton of Brontosaurus, may be seen in the American Museum of Natural History in New York City. Near them are the hipbones and tail of another Brontosaurus, with scars made by teeth of Allosaurus, which were found among the bones. Scientists at the museum have completed this story of ancient life by mounting an Allosaurus skeleton as if it were feeding on the plant-eater's remains.

DINOSAURS OF THE CHALK AGE

MIMUS walked along a sandy beach beside a swampy lake. Now and then he picked up a fish that had been washed ashore. Then he found a heap of sand that covered the eggs laid by a mother turtle. Mimus dug out the eggs and swallowed them without breaking their soft tough shells.

Mimus lived in a time often called the Chalk Age, because chalk was deposited in seas of North America and Europe. One of those seas covered part of the region where Long-tail, Brontosaurus and other large dinosaurs had lived millions of years before.

Mimus was a dinosaur too, but he was very different from other dinosaurs we have seen. He stood about nine feet tall, with a long neck and long legs which made him resemble an ostrich. His small head was birdlike, too, with beaks on the jaws instead of teeth. His full name, Ornithomimus (or′ ni tho my″ mus), means "bird mimic" or "a creature that looks like a bird."

Mimus, who looked like an ostrich, and the armored dinosaur.

When Mimus walked, he bobbed his head like a bird, and his feet made three-toed tracks in the sand. His plump body looked as if it would topple forward, but he balanced it with his tail which stuck out stiffly behind him. This was one way in which he did resemble the dinosaurs of ancient Arizona, and even big Allosaurus.

Although Mimus made use of his tail, it also was a

nuisance. It was so stiff that he often thumped it against trees, especially when he tried to dodge or turn quickly in the woods. Once Mimus broke its slender tip, which was even stiffer when it healed. Then a meat-eating dinosaur nipped it off in trying to capture Mimus. But the tip came off so easily that the birdlike dinosaur was able to run away.

Many months had gone by since that happened, and Mimus had forgotten about it. But he tried to stay in open places, and kept away from thickets in which meat-eating reptiles might hide. When something alarmed him he darted away without waiting to find out what it was.

· · · ·

Mimus was not alarmed, however, by grunts and thumping sounds that came from a tangle of reeds and bushes. These noises were made by an armored dinosaur that fed on plants and never attacked other reptiles.

The armored dinosaur was distantly related to Stegosaurus and was about sixteen feet long. Instead of being high and thin, however, his body was low and broad. His head and back were covered with thick bony plates, sharp spikes protected his sides, and his tail ended in a thick club. His jaws were covered with horny beaks with which he nipped stems and leaves from plants. These beaks were much more useful than his teeth, which were small and blunt.

Most meat-eating reptiles never tried to eat the armored dinosaur. But when one of them did attack him, he squatted down with his head close to his body and his legs tucked under his spikes. Only his tail stuck out, ready to swing from side to side, like an enormous war club. A few blows from it were enough to drive any other reptile away!

.   .   .   .

Soon after the armored dinosaur passed, Mimus heard another reptile splashing as it came from the lake. A duckbill dinosaur had swum into shallow water. In a moment it stood on its hind legs and walked along the shore.

The duckbill was almost twice as tall as Mimus and weighed many times as much. It could swim gracefully with its webbed feet but it walked clumsily, dragging its tail on the ground. Its head was long and stupid looking, and its jaws spread out into two broad beaks that looked like the beaks of a duck. It ate as a duck does, too, shoveling food up with its beaks. Hard things were crushed between small teeth that grew in closely packed rows near the back of the duckbill's mouth.

The duckbill dinosaur that walked past Mimus looked

Two duck-billed dinosaurs. The one with the crest actually lived long before his smooth-headed relative.

like the large one shown here. Other duckbills, which lived at different times and in different places, had heads of various shapes. In one the front of the skull was thickened, making the nose look "hooked." Another had a rounded crest of bone, and the crest of a third kind was divided. Strangest of all was a dinosaur whose crest extended like a curved feather on a hat.

When these queer bony structures were discovered scientists wondered how they were used. Then it was found that hollow tubes, called passages, from the nose went up into the crests and down to the reptiles' throats. When a crested dinosaur wanted to feed under water, he filled the passages with air and closed his nostrils. Then he breathed the air while his head was under water, shoveling a mouthful of food.

. . . .

When the duckbill went away, Mimus was left alone on the beach. By that time he felt sleepy, so he went to an open place and settled down for a nap. But he got up again when he heard a large heavy reptile coming toward the lake.

This new dinosaur was Triceratops (try sair' a tops), whose name means "three-horned head." Since one of the horns was on his nose we may call him Nose-horn for short.

Nose-horn was twenty-five feet long and ten feet tall, with a massive body and a thick tail that dragged on the ground when he walked. His skull was eight feet in length, but almost half of it was a wide bony frill that spread backward over the neck. Curved beaks covered

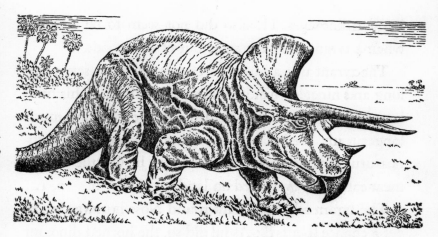

Triceratops, or Nose-horn, had armor that protected his neck.

the front of his jaws. The horn on his nose was short, but horns almost four feet long grew above his eyes.

As Nose-horn walked toward the lake he came to a big clump of ferns. He sniffed them two or three times, as if he wondered whether they really were good to eat. Then he nipped off their leaves with his beaks and crushed them between rows of small teeth that grew very close together. Those teeth were not made for real chewing but they did turn the leaves into pulp which Nose-horn could swallow easily.

Though Nose-horn ate plants he was not a timid, helpless creature like Mimus or the duckbill. Scars on his frill and sides showed that he had fought with other horned dinosaurs. He also did not seem to be alarmed when a tyrant dinosaur came out of the woods.

The tyrant was a huge, fierce creature forty-seven feet long and nineteen feet in height. He walked on his hind legs, like Allosaurus, but he had a larger head and much longer teeth. He is called the tyrant dinosaur, or Tyrannosaurus (ty ran" o saw' rus), because he was the biggest meat-eater that ever lived on land.

The tyrant began to walk round Nose-horn, trying to get a chance to attack. As he did so, the horned dinosaur turned, keeping his frill and horns toward his enemy. The frill made a shield for his neck and shoulders, and the horns were weapons which he could use if the tyrant attacked him.

Most dinosaurs would have given up, but the tyrant was too hungry and too stubborn to quit. He circled again and then rushed forward. His jaws snapped shut just a few inches from Nose-horn's back.

That was too far away for the teeth to do any harm, but not far enough for safety. Before the tyrant was able to dodge, Nose-horn lunged forward and lifted his head. His horns tore into the skin on the tyrant's left hind leg, and another quick thrust ripped into his side. The big meat-eater hissed with pain and began to back away.

Just then he caught sight of Mimus, standing timidly

on the beach. Here was something else to eat—something that had no shield and no dangerous horns. The tyrant rushed forward again, ready to make a kill.

Mimus could not fight such an enemy, but he could run away. For a moment he bobbed awkwardly, as if his body and tail did not balance. Then he "got his stride," and his slender legs worked so fast that they could hardly be seen. He darted along the beach so swiftly that the tyrant was left behind. After two or three minutes he stopped and then stalked into the woods.

Mimus soon had to stop, too, for his cool blood would not let him run long distances. He turned toward a thicket of rushes that was big enough to hide in, but too small to conceal enemies. There he halted and stood quite still. His dull colors matched the plants, and his slender neck and legs looked like three stems. Only his bright eyes showed plainly—but they were too small to be seen by any creature that was far away.

Mimus did not think about these things, or even decide to hide. But he did feel safe in the thicket. He would stay there while he rested and the tyrant went far away. Then he would come out and hunt another meal of dead fish or eggs.

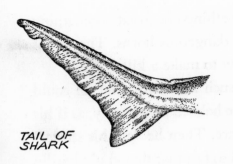

TAIL OF SHARK

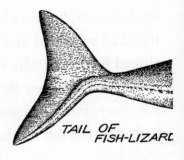

TAIL OF FISH-LIZARD

REPTILES OF ANCIENT SEAS

REPTILES came into existence on land, for they always breathe with lungs and their eggs cannot be laid in water. Yet some of them left the land to live in lakes, rivers and seas.

Grayback was a sea-dwelling, or marine, reptile that lived about 150 million years ago. This was during the age when Bronto and other huge dinosaurs waded in swamps of the West. Grayback's home was a sea that covered part of Europe, though some of his relatives have been found in North America.

Scientists call Grayback an ichthyosaur (ik′ thi o saur), which means "fish-lizard." This name is a very good one, for Grayback was a reptile that resembled a swordfish

64

Grayback, the fish-lizard, looked like a long-snouted shark.

or long-snouted shark. His body was torpedo shaped and his neck was too short to be seen. His legs had become finlike flippers, and there was a high, fleshy fin on his back. Only his eyes and tail were not sharklike. His eyes were round and very large. The backbone in his tail bent downward—not upward as it does in sharks.

. . . .

When we describe ancient animals we often have to work out the shape of their bodies from shells or skeletons. That is not necessary for fish-lizards, however, for many fossils contain films of carbon as well as teeth and petrified bones. Those films show the streamlined body, the flippers, the tail, and the tall fin on the back. The skin that covered the body was smooth with only a few scales on the flippers. Color grains show that the creatures were dark on the back, shading to white underneath. The dark color probably was dull green or bluish gray.

Most surprising of all are small skeletons inside those of full-grown reptiles. Those small skeletons are not remains of food, for they are neither crushed nor partly digested, and they lie far behind the stomach. They must be unhatched young ones which were killed and covered with mud when their mothers died.

This answers a question that once puzzled scientists. Fish-lizards could not creep on land, for their backbones were too weak and their flippers were useless for crawling. Yet their eggs could not be laid in water, like the eggs of amphibians. Mother fish-lizards solved this problem by keeping the eggs inside their bodies until the little ones hatched. Perhaps the mother also stayed with her young ones, finding food and protecting them until they could care for themselves.

. . . .

Grayback swam with his tail, using his flippers to balance himself, to turn, and to go upward or downward. He liked to skim along at the surface where he could breathe air through his nostrils, which were in front of his eyes. But he often dived and swam under water, especially when he was looking for food.

Grayback's favorite food was fish, which he caught with the small, sharp teeth in his slender jaws. He also ate creatures known as belemnites (be lem´ nites), which were related to our present-day squids and to Horn-shell. Instead of building shells outside their bodies they stiffened themselves with pointed structures called pens. In some formations belemnite pens are very common fossils.

As Grayback swam in the sea he often met other water reptiles. One, which we shall call Long-neck, had a long,

67

This American plesiosaur had a neck twenty-three feet long.

slender neck, a very wide body, and a tail which merely trailed behind his body. He swam with his legs, which were longer than Grayback's and were shaped like paddles, not fins.

Long-neck was a plesiosaur (plee' zi o saur), which

means "almost a lizard." This name fits some of its bones, but it does not describe the creature's appearance or habits. Long-neck did not look like a lizard, and he probably could not crawl out of water. There he swam at the surface or just below it, moving much more slowly than Grayback. Sometimes he held his neck high, with his head cocked to one side, so he could look for fish. When he saw one his neck swung toward it. *Snap!* went his long-toothed jaws, and the fish was caught.

Other "almost lizards" had shorter necks but long beaklike jaws. These reptiles probably swam much faster than Long-neck since they had to come close to a fish before they were able to catch it.

.　.　.　.

Although Long-neck and his neighbors lived in Europe other plesiosaurs spread around the world. One that lived where Australia is now was a gigantic reptile with a head nine feet long—about twice as big as the head of a tyrant dinosaur. Other large species lived in a sea that covered part of North America in the Chalk Age. One American species had a flat pointed head and a slender neck twenty-three feet in length.

Pictures once showed this creature's neck twisting to and fro like a snake. We now know that the neck was much too stiff for that. It could bend, but it could not twist or coil. It also could not dart out as a snake does when he strikes his prey.

Smaller American plesiosaurs often followed schools of fish that left the sea and began to swim up winding rivers. When the fish went from rivers to lakes the long-necked reptiles followed. Some even went into swampy bays where the water was deep enough for their bodies.

We don't know how many reptiles did this. We also don't know what they thought of the duckbill dinosaurs which they often met in the lakes. But we do know that some of the creatures remained in the lakes till they died, for their bones have been found in rocks that also contain remains of plant-eating dinosaurs.

Archelon, the giant turtle, kept a close watch for danger.

ADVENTURES OF ARCHELON

ARCHELON floated lazily in a pleasant bay. It was part of the Chalk-Age sea in which plesiosaurs went fishing about 100 million years ago.

Archelon (ar′ kee lon) was a turtle; a turtle that lived in the sea. Like many other ancient creatures she also was much larger than her relatives that live today. Her head

71

was about thirty inches long, and her broad shell measured eight feet from front to back. Her front flippers were six feet in length, and spread out like enormous paddles. They could take her swiftly through the water, but a slow movement now and then was enough to make her float.

Archelon's shell was not hard like that of many turtles. It was made of thick leathery skin spread over a framework of bone. Her ribs formed part of this framework, and her backbone ran down the middle. Her jaws were covered with sharp-edged beaks which curved like the beaks of an eagle.

Although Archelon seemed to be lazy, her eyes were open and she kept a sharp lookout for danger. She paid no attention to other turtles and was not alarmed by a plesiosaur that came paddling by. But she dived and tried to hide when she spied another reptile which we now call a mosasaur (moe′ sa saur).

Though the mosasaur was a reptile it looked like a huge thick-bodied eel more than twenty-five feet long. It had a flat pointed head, a streamlined body, and a flattened tail which it used for swimming. Its legs and feet had become broad paddles with webs of skin between the toes. Sharp teeth showed that it fed on fish and other reptiles.

*The mosasaur had a streamlined body, and its legs and feet
had become paddles.*

The mosasaur saw Archelon dive, but paid no more
attention to her. It was busy catching fish, which darted
one way and then another. Some even jumped out of the
water as they tried to get away from the mosasaur's jaws.

Archelon did not try to find out what the savage

reptile was doing. Down she went to the bottom of the bay, where she stirred up a cloud of mud as she stopped. When the mud settled it covered her shell and made her look like a low, broad mound.

The big turtle lay in the mud for hours, until she became hungry. Then she swam slowly under the water, looking for a meal. She was very fond of fish, though many fish swam so fast that she could not catch them. She also ate big thin-shelled oysters and creatures called ammonites (am' o nites), which were distant relatives of Horn-shell.

Archelon found some ammonites feeding on the remains of a fish. For two or three minutes she did not move; then she crept toward them very cautiously. Out came her big head and *snap!* went her jaws as she crushed a shell and swallowed the creature inside it. Another *snap!* and she swallowed a second ammonite— but all the rest were swimming away. They bobbed through the water shell-first, just as Horn-shell had done in more ancient times.

As the ammonites bobbed away, Archelon spied a bank of the large thin-shelled oysters. Since they could not escape she ate as many of them as she wanted. Then she went back to the surface and floated while the sunshine warmed her shell.

The big turtle floated for several hours until the sky became dark. Then she paddled across the bay to a place where the shore was a beach of white sand.

Other turtles also were swimming toward the beach but Archelon paid no attention to them. She paddled swiftly into shallow water and pulled herself onto the land. But her paddles were not built for crawling, and her shell dragged heavily. She took more than two hours to reach a ridge of sand so high that waves could not splash over it, even in a storm.

When Archelon came to the ridge she stopped crawling and began to dig. She scooped up sand with her front flippers and pushed it back under her body. Then she used her hind flippers to throw the sand out. In this way she soon dug a wide shallow pit, or nest, for her eggs.

Long before, when Archelon was young, she had laid only a dozen eggs at a time. But as years passed and she became larger she was able to lay more and more eggs. She put almost two hundred in this nest, arranging them in neat layers. Then she climbed out, covered them with sand and crawled away.

Archelon did not leave her nest and go straight into the bay. She crawled one way and another, and even went around in circles. Other turtles did the same. Soon they made a tangle of trails that would not help egg-eating reptiles, such as Mimus, find where the turtles had hidden their nests.

At last Archelon grew tired of crawling and went back to the sea. This was easier than coming up, though she splashed and struggled in order to reach water that was deep enough for swimming. Younger turtles did not have so much trouble, for they were not so large.

As soon as Archelon left the beach she forgot about her eggs. They would hatch in the sand without her help, and the young ones would crawl into the water as fast as they could go. There they would eat worms and other small creatures, and look out for themselves. Many would be eaten by fish, and some would be devoured by young reptiles or even by ammonites. Out of two hundred newly hatched turtles, only four or five might grow up and live long enough to lay eggs of their own.

That seems like a very small number, but Archelon and each of her relatives filled three or four nests with eggs, and did so every year. If four young ones from every nest grew up there would be plenty of giant turtles in the Chalk-Age sea.

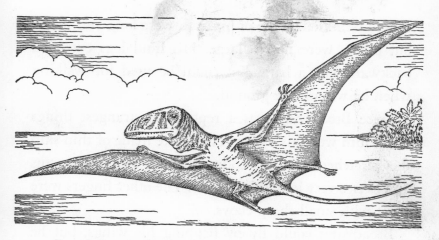

Broadwing looked for fish as he soared over the sea.

REPTILES THAT FLEW

BROADWING was flying above a warm, shallow sea. It covered northwestern Europe during the period, or age, when Grayback swam after fish and Brontosaurus waded in swamps. This means that Broadwing lived about 150 million years ago.

From a distance Broadwing looked a bit like a bird or bat, but he was a reptile about thirty-two inches long. His body was covered with bare skin, not feathers or fur, and he had a slender tail. His head was large and high but very narrow, and a patch of skin around each eye was deeply wrinkled. Some of his teeth were long and sharp, but others were not so large. His hind legs extended backward like a bat's, but could be used for walking when he was on the ground.

Since Broadwing was a reptile the strangest things about him were his wings. They were made of thin skin that stretched from his body and hind legs to his arms and to two very long thin fingers. The other fingers were short with small sharp claws.

Broadwing could fly by flapping his wings, but he preferred to soar. This means that he tilted his wings just right to make air currents carry him upward. Round and round he went, sometimes rising more than a hundred feet, and sometimes gliding down close to the water. He looked as if he were flying for fun, with his head cocked to one side so he could look down into the sea.

Broadwing probably did like to fly, but he did not do it for fun. While he soared he kept watch for shrimps and small fish, which often swam at the surface. When he saw one he tilted his wings and darted down to catch it. Then he spread his wings and began to soar again.

When the flying reptile swooped he took care not to splash into the sea. Many birds can dive, come back to the surface, and swim or fly away. But Broadwing was not as strong as a bird, and the skin on his wings did not shed water. If he had splashed into the sea he would have stayed there till he drowned.

Though Broadwing liked to fish he often alighted on beaches and ate things washed ashore by the waves. He walked awkwardly on all four feet, with his wings folded so the two long fingers were out of his way. He sometimes swallowed food as soon as he found it. At other times he kept it in a pouch of skin that hung down from his neck. This pouch was large enough to hold a good-sized meal.

· · · ·

We call flying reptiles pterosaurs (tair′ o saurz), which means "lizards with wings." The early ones resembled Broadwing, but as thousands and millions of years went by they changed in various ways. Some became as small as sparrows, but others grew very large. One group kept their long slender tails, but others had tails that grew shorter and shorter until they were only small stubs. Some short-tailed species had needle-shaped teeth. Others lost their teeth but developed sharp beaks with which they caught their food.

One of these beaked reptiles lived near the end of the Chalk Age and ranged from Europe to western North America. It often flew over the sea in which Archelon

Glider's wings spread as much as twenty-seven feet.

and mosasaurs swam. Its technical name means "flying reptile without teeth," but we may call it Glider for short.

Glider was a giant among pterosaurs. His wings had a spread of twenty-five feet to twenty-seven feet, or about four times as much as the wingspread of an eagle. His head was six to seven feet long, with a three-foot crest of bone that balanced the long beak. The crest also served as a rudder when Glider folded his wings and darted down to catch a fish.

In spite of Glider's big head and wide wings he was not very heavy. His body was twenty-four inches long and weighed twenty-five pounds, or only twice as much as an eagle. The long bones in his wings were hollow and were filled with air. The solid part of bones two or three feet long was no thicker than a piece of blotting paper!

This huge Chalk-Age pterosaur probably rested in the tops of trees that grew near the edge of the sea. There Glider was able to sit or hang by his hind feet, with his head downward. On stormy days he stayed at home, for a very strong wind would have blown him far out to sea. On fine days he waited till sunshine warmed his body. Then he flapped his wings until he was high enough to soar. His muscles were so strong that he could flap his wings many times without becoming tired.

As Glider soared over the sea he often saw Archelon and long-necked plesiosaurs. Since they were much too large to be eaten he kept on going until he sighted a fish. When it came to the surface he darted down and caught it between his beaks.

Like Broadwing and other flying reptiles Glider kept the fish he caught in a pouch that hung down below his throat. But at last the pouch became so full that it could hold no more. Glider then found air currents that took him aloft and carried him back to land. There he alighted on a tree and began to eat his meal. He did not go out to sea again until the last fish was digested and he had had a long rest.

These ancient birds had teeth, and fingers on their wings.

BIRDS THAT HAD TEETH

AS Broadwing flew home to rest in a treetop he often saw some of the world's first birds.

Those birds were smaller than crows and were closely related to reptiles. Their heads were covered with wrinkled skin, and their jaws had scales instead of beaks. When they opened their mouths to eat or scream they showed more than forty small teeth.

Other things about these birds were almost as strange

as their teeth. They had hairlike feathers on the head and neck, but small feathers that covered the body were not much more than scales. The wings were blunt and had three small "fingers," and the tail contained bones all the way to the tip. Feathers grew along each side of the tail instead of spreading out like a fan. Except for its feathers that long tail might have belonged to a lizard.

· · · ·

The toothed, reptilelike birds roosted in trees that grew near the seashore. The creatures could perch as birds do now, but they probably could not hop from one branch to another. When they wanted to move through the trees they crawled, using the fingers on their wings as well as their four-toed feet. Those fingers could catch hold of twigs and the stems of big leaves on trees called cycads (sy′ kads), which resembled palms.

The birds probably climbed to catch insects and small reptiles that also lived in trees. For longer journeys the birds flapped their wings to get into the air and then glided to bushes or open beaches. There they walked about awkwardly, picking up dead animals washed ashore by waves. They probably ate anything they could catch or find.

Since the toothed birds could not fly very well they did

Diver's legs were near his tail, where they made fine paddles.

not soar hour after hour, as Broadwing did when he went fishing. But the birds sometimes were caught in strong stormy winds that carried them far out to sea. When they tried to fly back to land they became so tired that they fell into the water and drowned.

The reason that we feel sure this happened is that fossil birds have been found in thin beds of limestone that settled on the sea bottom. This limestone also contains fossil shrimps, horseshoe crabs, jellyfish and other marine creatures. It even contains flying reptiles that drowned when they swooped too low while they were catching fish.

As millions of years went by, toothed birds traveled from Europe to other parts of the world. Some of them also changed greatly. While old-fashioned kinds died out new ones lost their lizardlike tails and developed beaks.

Several of these new toothed birds lived in North America during the Chalk Age. The largest and strangest was Hesperornis (hes″ per or′ nis). This name means "western bird," but "Diver" gives a better idea of this creature's appearance and habits.

Diver was a big bird, almost five feet long. He had a large head, long beaks, and teeth that slanted backward. His neck was slender and his body was streamlined like a torpedo. He had no wings and could not even walk, for his legs were close to his tail. He would have toppled over if he had tried to take a step.

But Diver did not try to walk, for he did not need to. His home was a pleasant bay in the Chalk-Age sea where he could swim and dive. He was built just right for this, with his slender body and big webbed feet, which made powerful paddles. They sent him skimming over the surface or drove him swiftly through the water when he dived for food.

Diver liked to swim lazily in his bay, moving his feet just often enough to keep his body from sinking. But when he felt hungry he swam faster, tipping his head from side to side so he could look into the water. As soon as he saw a fish he dived, caught it between his beaks, and came back to the surface. There he swallowed the fish and began to look for more.

When spring came Diver found a mate who probably looked just like him. Some scientists think the big birds wriggled out of the water and onto the shore, where they built a simple nest on the ground. Others think Diver and his mate built a floating nest of mud and dead plants, fastening it to rushes that grew in very shallow water. The big birds could build a floating nest much more easily than they could make one on land.

This is only a supposition, of course, for no one has ever found the nest or eggs of Hesperornis. But birds called grebes (greebs) now build floating nests, even though they are able to fly and can walk clumsily on land. Why shouldn't the Divers, who could not walk, also build their nest in the bay where they lived and caught fish?

CYNO, A BEAST-REPTILE

BIRDS are not the only things that developed, or are descended, from reptiles. Reptiles also produced the creatures with hair or fur and warm blood whose proper name is mammals (mam′ alz). We often call them "beasts" or just "animals."

Cyno (sy′ no) was one of the links between reptiles and beasts. He was not a "missing link," however, for his skeleton has been found in South Africa. It shows that he lived there during the age when Long-jaw and small dinosaurs made their homes in Arizona.

Cyno did not resemble either Long-jaw or a dinosaur. He was a reptile about four feet in length with sturdy legs that kept his body up above the ground. He had a pointed nose, or snout, but the back of his head was large. The muscles that worked his jaws were thick and very strong.

Cyno's teeth showed that he was not an ordinary reptile. The teeth of most reptiles are almost alike, but Cyno had short biting teeth in front and then two pairs of long

Cyno, a beast-reptile, walked to a rocky hill.

"canines." Behind these came broad cutting and chewing teeth that looked like those of dogs. They explained why scientists have named this creature Cynognathus (sy′ nog nath″ us), which means "dog-jaw."

There are many other ways in which Cyno was not an ordinary reptile. The top, or roof, of his mouth was beastlike, and so was the one large bone that formed most of each lower jaw. The joint between his skull and neck was double, as it is in cats and dogs. Other beastlike structures are found in his backbone, shoulders, hips and legs. His skin probably was scaly, but some of the scales may have been long and slender, which meant that they were turning into hairs.

One morning Cyno came out of the woods and walked

to a rocky hill. There he stopped to look and listen. Something was making a noise among the ferns that grew upon the hillside. The noisy creature might be good to eat, and Cyno was very hungry.

Many reptiles would have found a place to hide, and would have waited till the other animal came near them. Then they would have pounced upon it. That was the way Finback and some dinosaurs hunted, and they were many times as big and as powerful as Cyno.

But Cyno was more active than Finback, and he was too hungry to wait. Besides, the noisy creature might lie down to rest, or it might wander into a valley where trees, ferns and vines grew so thickly that Cyno could not go through them. If it did that, the hungry beast-reptile would miss a chance for a meal.

Of course, Cyno did not bother to think all this out. He just listened and sniffed for a few seconds and began to walk down the hill. He tried not to make a noise, and he stayed behind rocks and ferns that kept him from being seen. This meant that Cyno was stalking his prey, not just going along and hoping to catch a meal.

At last Cyno saw the other reptile—but he did not rush upon it. Instead, he stopped and blinked his eyes, as if he did not know what to do. If his face had not been too dull he might have looked disappointed.

For what Cyno saw was one of his own distant relatives. It was six feet long, with a big head, a stubby tail and a very thick body. Its wrinkled skin was tough and thick, and a bony crest protected its neck. The heavy jaws had lost their teeth, but the creature nipped off

The beaked reptile opened his mouth and turned to face Cyno.

ferns with powerful beaks. It could also use those beaks to slash anything that attacked it.

Cyno seemed to know that, for he did not attack. He began to walk around the other reptile. He was looking for a chance to rush at it and give a bite that would kill it before it could use its beak.

Although Cyno tried to be quiet, the beaked reptile heard him. It raised its head and grunted fiercely. When it saw Cyno, it turned to face him. As he circled around it kept on turning, with its beaks open and ready to bite. It grunted again and again as if it were saying, "Stay back!"

Round and round went the two reptiles, grunting and glaring at each other. Cyno did not dare to attack, and he did not want to give up. But finally his legs grew tired, and his dull brain realized that he could not win. He backed away from the beaked reptile, turned, and then scrambled up the hill. As the beaked reptile saw him go it began to eat fern leaves again.

.   .   .   .

Cyno climbed the hill slowly, poking his nose into clumps of ferns and under slabs of stone. In this way he caught several big roaches. He also snapped up two small amphibians that lived on land instead of in water. They looked and acted like our present-day salamanders.

Such food was good, but there wasn't much of it. Cyno was hungrier than ever, and hunger made him bad tempered. When he saw another beast-reptile, he grunted and snapped at it. The other reptile grunted too, but it kept one foot on a creature which it had just killed.

As soon as Cyno saw the fresh meat, he rushed at the other beast-reptile. They came together with a thud and began to slash with their long canine teeth. Cyno cut a long gash in his enemy's shoulder, and it tore the skin on Cyno's neck. Both pushed and clawed at each other with their five-toed feet.

They fought for almost ten minutes, which was a long time for a quarrel between two reptiles. At last Cyno gave a push which sent his enemy sprawling. Cyno slashed out once more and then pounced upon the meat. Holding it down with both front feet, he tore a big bite from it, and then raised his head. The other reptile glared at him but it did not attack. Instead it turned and stumbled down the rocky hill.

Cyno watched his defeated enemy go and took another bite. He cut it off with broad teeth at the side of his mouth, but instead of gulping it down, he chewed it with teeth still farther back in his jaws. That was a dog-like way of eating, but it seemed quite right for a reptile that was *almost* a beast.

Fen, or Phenacodus, had a very long tail.

EARLY BEASTS AND DAWN-HORSES

TRUE mammals developed soon after Cyno lived in Africa. Perhaps they resembled him, though they probably were smaller. They had warm blood, of course, and were covered with hair, not scales.

The first mammals wandered about, and so did those that developed later. They spread across Africa to Europe and Asia, and then to North America. Yet they did not grow large or become very common. Some scientists think this was because dinosaurs and other reptiles constantly preyed upon them. Only small beasts that lived in thick woods or even in trees could escape those hungry reptiles.

This is only a theory, and it may not be right. But we know that mammals remained small and scarce as long as reptiles were very common. Then the savage reptiles died out, and hairy beasts became plentiful during the age that followed. In fact, they became so important that we often call this new division of earth history the Age of Mammals.

Phenacodus (fe nak′ o dus), which we shall call Fen, was one of the beasts that lived early in the Age of Mammals. He was almost as tall as a sheep, but weighed a good deal less. He had a narrow head and a long, thick tail that dragged on the ground when he walked. From a distance he looked rather like a big cat, but his toes had small hoofs instead of claws. His teeth also were not catlike, but were broad and blunt. Such teeth could be used only for eating plants.

Fen lived on prairies in the West, where Nose-horn and Mimus had roamed during the latter part of the Chalk Age. Instead of going about alone, as they did, Fen led a herd of animals just like himself. The herd walked about, feeding upon small plants, and it often rested in the shade on sunny afternoons. There one or two animals kept watch while the others dozed.

94

Coryphodon used his tusks if crocodiles attacked his young ones.

Once every day Fen and his herd went to a river to drink. The river was broad and swampy, with thickets along its banks. Fen always stopped to sniff and listen for danger before the herd walked through those thickets. He knew that carnivores, or meat-eating beasts, often hid there, waiting to pounce on plant-eaters and kill them.

Some of those carnivores were large clumsy animals with broad heavy heads. They often fed upon animals that had died of old age. Another kind was much smaller, but more dangerous. It also had a large head, but its body was slender, its legs were short, and its tail was very long. It probably swam like our present-day otter, catching fish and soft-shelled turtles for food. But it also hunted on land, where it captured young animals that wandered away from their parents. It had killed two or three young ones belonging to Fen's own herd.

The largest beast that lived among thickets is now called Coryphodon (ko rif' o don). He looked rather like a long lean hippopotamus with a flat head and thick legs. His feet, however, resembled those of an elephant.

Although Coryphodon ate plants, four of his teeth had grown into thick, sharp tusks. He used them when he fought other Coryphodons, or when crocodiles attacked his young ones in the swampy river. For Coryphodons liked the water, and often swam or waded about, eating juicy plants. This gave crocodiles a chance to seize young animals and pull their heads under water, where they quickly drowned.

. . . .

When Fen rested in open woods he often saw herds of beasts about as large as cats. Their heads were large, their backs were curved and their legs were very slender. They had four toes on each front foot, but only three behind.

These little creatures were dawn-horses; we often call them Eohippus (ee" o hip' us), though they have still another name. They lived in herds, just as Fen did, but

Dawn-horses had four toes in front and three behind.

they spent most of their time in the woods, not on open prairies. They ate tender plants instead of grass, for their teeth were not thick enough to chew tough gritty food. Besides, grass was not common in the days when dawn-horses lived.

But why do we call them *horses?* Do they really deserve that name?

They do, for thousands of fossils connect these ancient beasts with the horses that live today. Those fossils show that dawn-horses and their relatives changed in many ways and many, many times. They grew larger and larger, with longer necks, and their backs grew straight instead of curved. They also developed long strong legs, lost all except one toe on each foot, and covered it with a large hoof. Their teeth became so thick and so solid that they could chew the toughest grass.

Dawn-horses alone did not do all this; they only made a start. A few of them had colts that grew larger than their parents or had some smaller toes. These colts had young ones that changed still more, and so on through millions of years. As new creatures developed old ones died out. Dawn-horses were only fossils long before the first "true" horses began to walk on feet with only one toe.

In fact, dawn-horses died out only a few million years after Fen saw them running about in the woods and nibbling tender plants. They were followed by beasts that had changed just a little, and then by some that had changed a lot more. The next horses we shall see were larger and swifter, and their front feet had three toes instead of four. They also lived at a later time, among animals that were very different from Fen and Coryphodon.

BEASTS OF THE BADLANDS

CHOO! Choo-oo! snorted Titan. Insects were buzzing around his nose. He snorted and shook his head to make them go away.

Titan lived about 35 million years ago, which was long after Fen, Coryphodon and dawn-horses died out. His home was in western South Dakota, but animals related to him have been found in many other regions. Some of them even roamed across Asia and into eastern Europe.

Titan looked like a huge rhinoceros with two blunt horns that grew side by side, not one behind the other. Still, his teeth and bones were so different from those of a rhino that we call him a titanothere (ty' tan o theer). This means "giant beast," and Titan deserved his name. He was about thirteen feet long and seven feet tall, and he weighed more than many modern circus elephants.

After Titan drove the insects away he began to feel hungry. The prairie around him was covered with short grass, and tall marsh grass grew beside many streams and

Titan looked like a rhinoceros but was larger than many elephants.

ponds. But the big titanothere's teeth were not made for grinding such tough gritty food, so he ate leaves of weed-like plants and bushes. He pulled the leaves into his mouth with his long upper lip.

Many other "giant beasts" also were eating leaves or

browsing. Some of them looked like Titan and were members of his herd. Others were smaller and had shorter horns or heads of different shapes. They belonged to other kinds, or species (spee′ shees), and lived in separate herds.

Titan and his herd walked along while they were eating, until they came to a stream. There all the large animals drank, and most of them waded into the water. Young ones, or calves, stayed on the bank. Some lay down to rest, but others played while their mothers were wading.

The cool water felt so good that the titanotheres waded and splashed for almost an hour. But when a calf bleated in fright the full-grown animals stopped playing.

The calf bleated because it saw two hungry carnivores. They looked just a little like wolves, but their bodies were thick, their legs were clumsy and their heads were very large. They generally ate dead creatures, but they killed living ones when they could. Just then they were stalking the titanothere calf. With good luck they could rush out and kill it while its mother was in the stream.

But the calf's mother heard it bleat and splashed back to the bank. Up she came with her head held low and her horns near the ground. She tossed one carnivore into the air and trampled on him when he came down. The other

One of the carnivores that tried to kill a titanothere calf.

one turned and ran away, as fast as his clumsy legs could take him.

After drinking and wading, the titanotheres browsed for an hour or two. But by that time the sunshine was hot, so the herd went to a grove of oak trees and lay down in the shade. Only Titan himself did not lie down. He stood up and kept watch while the other animals slept.

As Titan stood guard he heard and smelled many other animals. He did not see most of them, for his eyes were small and poor. Things as far away as one of our blocks disappeared or seemed to be shadows when he looked at them.

One creature that Titan did see plainly was a land-dwelling tortoise. It was a big one with a thick, rough

These three-toed horses were much larger than dawn-horses.

shell, and it stopped to nip leaves from a plant near one of Titan's feet. Then it walked away through the woods.

Soon after the tortoise disappeared, a herd of the three-toed horses came to the woods. They were at least twice as tall as the dawn-horse, yet they seemed very small when they stood near Titan. They also were very timid, and were ready to run away at the slightest strange noise.

.   .   .   .

Would you like to see the region where these ancient animals lived? You may do so in the Badlands of South Dakota, which lie near a range of mountains known as the Black Hills.

Of course, you will find that the country has changed since Titan and his neighbors lived there. The low, moist prairie has become a high plain with wheat fields and "rangeland," or natural pastures. You will see horses, cattle and jackrabbits, and will find bright yellow sunflowers nodding beside the road.

You will also find that the ground Titan walked on has been covered by clay and soft sandstone. The sand-

Rainwater has worn the Badlands into steep ridges and peaks.

stone settled in rivers, but the clay was spread out on ancient prairies when streams overflowed. It is gray, brown, pink, and cream-colored, and is as much as seven hundred feet thick.

Though the weather is dry much of the time, rains sometimes fall very hard. Rain water has worn into the clay, making gullies, canyons and wide valleys. The clay that has not been worn away forms ridges and thin sharp peaks. Pioneers who tried to ride among those ridges had such a hard time that they called the region Badlands. Although there are many other badlands, these are the most famous in North America.

No one knows how many fossils are covered by clays and sandstones in the Badlands. Collectors have found thousands of skulls and skeletons, and have sent them to museums in many parts of the world. If you look carefully you may pick up a piece of turtle shell or the bone of a beast that lived on the ancient prairie. You may even find a brown-and-white tooth, so big you will know it belonged to a titanothere.

But even if you don't find a fossil, you need not be disappointed. You will see the Badlands themselves, with their layers of clay that settled on land and their sandstone that filled wide, shallow rivers. Best of all, you can imagine what they were like in ancient times, when little horses ran on three toes and beasts as big as elephants rested under trees.

SOME AMERICAN CAMELS

MODERN camels are large beasts with humps on their backs and thick pads on their feet. Two kinds, or species, live in Asia and Africa, and some of their relatives, which have no humps, are found in South America. Most of us never see them except when we go to circuses and zoos.

Though the camel family now lives in other parts of the world, it began in North America. Its first members were not much larger than rabbits, and they appeared in the West soon after Fen and Coryphodon lived there. These early creatures (they were not real camels) had long hind legs with two-toed hind feet, though each front foot had four toes. The animals probably looked and acted a good deal like dawn-horses.

Other members of the camel family made their homes in Nebraska and South Dakota soon after Titan lived there. These animals were as tall as a sheep, but were not so large. They had long slim necks, small bodies and

This ancient member of the camel family had no hump and was only about as tall as a sheep. Its fossils have been found in Nebraska and South Dakota.

slender legs. They ran about on two-toed feet, with small hoofs instead of pads. We think they grazed, or fed on grass, as well as on tender leaves.

· · · ·

The camel family became really common about 25 million years ago. Some kinds looked like little antelope, with slender legs and feet. They lived in huge herds that wandered over grassy plains. At night they lay down to sleep, and those that were old or sick died before morning came. One ancient "bed ground" contained bones of a hundred animals that died in this way.

Long-toes was about nine feet tall.

Another kind of camel, which was much larger, has been given a name that means "Long-toes." He might have been called "Long-legs" or "Long-neck," and he also had a long, slender head.

Long-toes was about nine feet tall when he stood up and raised his neck. His feet had two toes with slender sharp hoofs which carried most of his weight when he walked or ran across grassy plains.

This tall camel could find plenty of grass, but he did not eat it. His food was the leaves of low trees and tall bushes. He could reach the leaves easily, pulling them off with his lips instead of biting them. When he wanted some leaves that were especially high, he reared up on his hind legs to reach them. He filled his mouth as fast as he could and then chewed the leaves when he stood on all four feet again.

Another camel, which lived at a later time, was even taller than Long-toes. It must have looked almost like a giraffe as it walked about browsing on trees. But when it drank it did not spread its legs and then bend them as giraffes now do. The giraffe-camel's neck was so long that it could get its head down to water without any trouble, even when it was standing erect.

Most carnivores of that time were slow and clumsy, and the tall giraffe-camels easily ran away from them. The camels also defended themselves by striking (not kicking) with their forefeet. Their long, sharp hoofs were dangerous weapons, as every meat-eating animal knew.

. . . .

Since camels began in North America, you may wonder how they got to other continents. Did they make

This creature had such a long neck that we call it a giraffe-camel.

long hard journeys from one part of the earth to another? Or did they find some easier way?

Camels went from our continent to others just by roaming about instead of staying at home. While the tall giraffe-camels were living, others with shorter necks and legs began to wander away from the region now known as western Nebraska. Some animals went northward and some wandered southward. Those that went northward kept on going until they came to Alaska, and then crossed a strip of land that connected Alaska with Asia. Camels that wandered southward crossed Mexico and the Isthmus of Panama, and then began to spread out through South America.

Of course, no single camel walked from western Nebraska to Asia or South America. Some camels went fifty or a hundred miles and had young ones that went fifty or a hundred miles farther. This happened again and again, during thousands or even millions of years. The animals that reached South America were more than great-great-great-grandchildren of those that left Nebraska. To give the correct relationship between them, we'd have to add more "greats" than this page would hold.

As camels wandered to other continents they also changed greatly. Those that went to Asia grew humps on their backs and thick pads on their feet. Their descendants that reached Africa grew taller, but developed only one hump. Humps contain fat which the animals use when they cannot get enough food.

South American camels also developed pads on their feet, but they did not grow humps. Except for their feet, they looked like many of the camels that lived in the prehistoric West. But none of them is as tall as Long-toes or the great giraffe-camels that came after him.

You probably have one more question, but it cannot be answered. No one knows why camels still live on other continents, but died out where they began, in North America. We only know that they made their homes here for millions of years, but then became scarce and finally disappeared. The last ones died just a few thousand years ago, for their skulls, with dry flesh on the bones, have been found in western caves.

Though Glypto was a beast, he looked like a huge turtle.

GLYPTO AND OTHER BEASTS
OF THE PAMPAS

WHEN camels went to South America they crossed the Isthmus of Panama. But they could not have done that in earlier times, for the ocean cut South America off from other continents.

When one land is separated from others, strange animals generally develop. That has happened in Australia, where mammals related to opossums have become long-legged kangaroos and koalas (ko ah′ las), which look like teddy bears. It also happened in ancient South America, and the strange beasts that developed kept on living after the sea disappeared. In fact they lived and developed for millions of years after camels, horses and other mammals began to come down from the North.

.   .   .   .

Glypto was one of the strangest of all South American mammals. He looked like an enormous turtle, with a shell five to six feet long. This shell was made of small bones fastened together. Bony rings covered part of the tail, which ended in a heavy club armed with bony spikes.

This tail reminds us of Stegosaurus, but teeth and bones in the skeleton prove that Glypto was a mammal. His full name was glyptodont (glip′ toe dahnt), and he was related to a small shell-covered beast known as the armadillo (ar″ ma dil′ o). There were armadillos when Glypto was alive, and one species now makes its home in Mexico and southern Texas.

Some glyptodonts also went to North America, crossing the Isthmus of Panama and then wandering northward. But the kind with spikes on his tail was too slow and lazy to go very far. He stayed at home, in the region now called the Pampas (pam′ pas), in the country of Argentina.

Glypto's blunt head shows that he was a peaceful creature that had teeth which he used to chew coarse grass. He walked about on four stubby legs that ended in broad blunt feet. He probably slept a great deal, and never traveled more than three or four miles from the place in which he was born. Even when bears and saber-toothed "cats" came near, Glypto did not run away. Instead, he crouched on the ground and tucked his head close to his shell. No sabertooth could slash his neck, and only a few young, foolish bears came near Glypto's tail. When they did, one blow from those sharp spikes was enough to drive them away.

.   .   .   .

Most of the mammals Glypto met paid no attention to him. But sometimes, when he went to drink, a Toxodon (tox' o don) would grunt angrily, as if it thought he should not come near. Beasts with long snouts also snorted with anger if Glypto waddled past and woke them from a nap.

Toxodon was as big as a rhinoceros, which means that he weighed almost three tons. But he looked more like a hippopotamus, though his head was not so large or so wide as the head of a hippo. Actually, Toxodon belonged to a group of mammals that developed in South America and never went north of the Isthmus of Panama.

Toxodon and Long-snout.

They could walk on land, but not very fast, and they spent much of their time swimming or wading in rivers and swampy lakes.

The long-snouted beasts also belonged to a special South American group. Long-snout himself was eight feet tall and as big as any present-day camel. His head was short, but his neck and legs were long, and his three-

This shaggy ground sloth was about twenty feet long.

toed feet had hoofs. He ate leaves which he pulled from trees with his snout, but his teeth showed that he also chewed grass. Still, he did not care for grass so coarse as the kinds on which Glypto fed.

. . . .

One morning as Glypto walked toward the river he met a herd of ground sloths. They were huge beasts, eighteen to twenty feet long, covered with shaggy hair. Their heads were big and their bodies were bigger, and their legs were thick. They walked on the outer edges of

A saber-toothed "cat" was stalking the ground sloths.

their feet and were so awkward that they looked as if they were going to roll over every time they took a step.

The ground sloths had long powerful claws but they were as peaceful as Glypto. They seldom quarreled among themselves, and they stayed near groves of trees that were common on the ancient Pampas. When a ground sloth felt hungry it sat up on its hind legs, bracing itself with its tail. Then it pulled branches down to its mouth and munched their leaves. Sometimes it broke branches that were too stiff to bend.

On that morning a hungry saber-toothed "cat" was stalking the herd of ground sloths. This great carnivore was as large as a lion, though he had a short tail. His forelegs were very thick and strong, and so was his neck. When he snarled he showed dagger-shaped canine teeth almost eight inches long.

Sabertooth slipped through the grass till he came to a ground sloth that was eating leaves. Then the carnivore leaped forward. His claws dug into the ground sloth's skin, while his teeth stabbed into its back.

If the sloth had been down on all fours those stabbing teeth would have killed it. But the animal was sitting up, and its forefeet with their claws were free. It turned and struck with one foot and then the other, ripping Sabertooth's sides with long claws. Before the catlike beast could jump back the sloth struck again, even harder than before.

That was the end of the fight, for Sabertooth limped away. Glypto squatted down for safety, but he did not have to do so. The big carnivore was too badly hurt to do any more hunting. All he wanted was to find a place where he could lie under shady trees until his wounds were healed.

SHAG, AN ICE-AGE ELEPHANT

SHAG walked lazily across a sunny meadow. Now and then he stopped to watch his neighbors or to pull a bunch of grass with his trunk. Sometimes he ate the grass and sometimes he threw it into the air and let it fall upon his head.

Shag was a woolly mammoth, a kind of elephant that was common during the last great Ice Age. Woolly mammoths lived in France and other countries of Europe, and in northern Asia. They also roamed across Alaska and Canada and the northern half of the United States. The meadow where Shag was pulling grass was part of the region we now call Illinois.

Although Shag is known as a mammoth, he was no larger than many circus elephants. This means that he was about nine feet high at the shoulder and weighed about four tons.

Still, Shag did not look like a circus elephant. His skin was covered with grayish wool and shaggy brown hair

Shag had a large head and long, curved tusks that came almost as high as his eyes.

instead of being bare like the skin of modern elephants. His big head was higher than his shoulders, and his hind legs were short. Two long tusks curved upward, almost as high as his eyes.

We often think of the Ice Age as a time when huge

glaciers spread from the North, covering the land with ice hundreds or thousands of feet in thickness. That did happen again and again, killing some animals and making others find new homes that were far away from the glaciers. But there also were times when the glaciers melted and the climate became warm. Then animals came north again, as soon as grass, bushes and trees began to grow on the land that had been covered with ice.

Woolly mammoths were common all through the Ice Age, even when climates were cold. But Shag and his neighbors lived during a warm time that began more than 200 thousand years ago and lasted 100 thousand years. In the summer the mammoths ate grass that grew on meadows and rested in shady groves on hot afternoons. When winter came the big animals fed upon moss and branches which they broke from trees. Their thick wool kept them warm, while their coarse hair kept rain and snow from wetting their skins.

Since the mammoths were elephants, they lived in a herd. It was led by an old grandmother who decided when the herd should go from one meadow to another and when it should stop to rest.

As Shag roamed about with the herd he often met other animals with trunks and tusks, known as mastodons (mass' toe dons). Their foreheads were low and

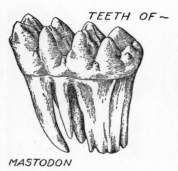

TEETH OF ~

MASTODON

MAMMOTH

sloping, their grinding teeth were smaller and thinner than those of real elephants, and their tusks were not curved so much as Shag's.

Mastodons and mammoths also had different ways of living. Mammoths liked groves and grassy meadows, and they seldom went to swamps or rivers unless they wanted to drink. Mastodons often stayed in thick forests, but they also were fond of swampy places where they could wade in water or walk in deep, soft mud. They often went to bogs to eat, even though plenty of plants grew upon dry land.

One morning as Shag came for a drink, he saw a mastodon wade into a bog. Farther and farther it went, till the water came high around its body. Then it stopped to eat plants which it pulled up with its trunk.

When the mastodon finished its meal, it tried to go

Mastodons had low foreheads and their tusks were not very much curved.

back to the forest. But its feet and legs were so deep in the mud that it could not pull them out. The harder it tried to do so, the deeper and faster it sank.

The mastodon struggled and screamed, but it could not get out of the bog. Soon it vanished under the water, where its hair and flesh slowly decayed while its bones and teeth were covered with mud. There they lay for thousands of years, finally becoming fossils that were not petrified. Bits of half-chewed plants between the teeth showed what the animal was eating just before it died.

The long-horned bison dared other beasts to come and fight.

One day the mammoth herd took a trip that was much longer than usual. The mammoths crossed meadows on which deer and antelopes were feeding, and passed ponds where beasts that looked like huge beavers were swimming. In one grove the mammoths met several ground sloths, which grumbled as they got out of the way. These sloths had long claws and shaggy hair, but they were not so large as the one that had fought Sabertooth in South America.

At last the mammoths crossed a prairie where a herd

of bison was grazing. The animals looked like our present-day bison, but were larger and had longer horns. The horns of one big fellow were six feet from tip to tip.

Two of the bison began to fight, and Shag stopped to watch them. At first the angry beasts bellowed and pawed the ground, as if they were trying to frighten each other. Then they lowered their heads and charged. Shag heard a dull *Thud!* as they came together.

Round and round the bison went, pushing and goring each other with their horns. At last one of them was hurt so badly that it fell to its knees. As soon as it could get up, it turned and limped away. The victor pawed the ground and bellowed, as if it were daring other beasts to come and fight.

Shag heard the challenge but paid no attention, for he knew it was not meant for him. Besides, the rest of the mammoth herd had kept on going across the prairie while he was watching the fight. Since Shag did not want to be left behind, he trotted after the others. Soon he was back in his proper place, where he could drive away any wolf or bear that tried to come near one of the calves.

For More Information

Booklets about "prehistoric" animals and plants are published by the American Museum of Natural History, New York 24, N.Y., the Chicago Museum of Natural History, the Denver Museum of Natural History, and the Los Angeles Museum. Illustrated articles often appear in the magazine *Natural History,* published by the American Museum. The following books also contain a great deal of information:

America Before Man, by Elizabeth C. Baity. Viking Press. A large book with many drawings and photographs.

Animals of Yesterday, by Bertha M. Parker. Row, Peterson & Company. Mostly about reptiles and mammals. Not all the colored pictures are good.

Before the Dawn of History, by Charles R. Knight. McGraw-Hill Book Company. Written for adults; many large pictures.

The Book of Prehistoric Animals, by Raymond L. Ditmars and Helene Carter. J. B. Lippincott Company. Colored picture maps show where ancient vertebrates lived.

The Dinosaur Book, by Edwin H. Colbert. McGraw-Hill Book Company. A fine well-illustrated book about ancient reptiles in general; for readers of high-school age and adults.

Life Long Ago: The Story of Fossils, by Carroll Lane Fenton. The John Day Company. The story of plant and animal life through 600 million years, written for young readers. There are 156 illustrations in color and black-and-white.

Life Through the Ages, by Bertha M. Parker. Row, Peterson & Company. A small book with colored pictures; describes animals without backbones as well as vertebrates.

Our Earth and Its Life, by Mary G. Phillips and Julia M. Wright. D. C. Heath & Company. Contains fourteen short chapters on ancient plants and animals.

Other Books About Nature and Science

4088